WOMEN IN SCIENCE & TECHNOLOGY

Annie EASLEY

BY M.M. EBOCH

ILLUSTRATED BY ELENA BIA

Rourke
Educational Media
rourkeeducationalmedia.com

A Division of
Carson Dellosa
Education

Before Reading: *Building Background Knowledge and Vocabulary*

Building background knowledge can help children process new information and build upon what they already know. Before reading a book, it is important to tap into what children already know about the topic. This will help them develop their vocabulary and increase their reading comprehension.

Questions and Activities to Build Background Knowledge:

1. Look at the front cover of the book and read the title. What do you think this book will be about?
2. What do you already know about this topic?
3. Take a book walk and skim the pages. Look at the table of contents, photographs, captions, and bold words. Did these text features give you any information or predictions about what you will read in this book?

Vocabulary: *Vocabulary Is Key to Reading Comprehension*

Use the following directions to prompt a conversation about each word.

- Read the vocabulary words.
- What comes to mind when you see each word?
- What do you think each word means?

Vocabulary Words:
- *barriers*
- *bias*
- *code*
- *counseled*
- *degree*
- *hybrid*
- *opinions*
- *research*

During Reading: *Reading for Meaning and Understanding*

To achieve deep comprehension of a book, children are encouraged to use close reading strategies. During reading, it is important to have children stop and make connections. These connections result in deeper analysis and understanding of a book.

 Close Reading a Text

During reading, have children stop and talk about the following:

- Any confusing parts
- Any unknown words
- Text to text, text to self, text to world connections
- The main idea in each chapter or heading

Encourage children to use context clues to determine the meaning of any unknown words. These strategies will help children learn to analyze the text more thoroughly as they read.

When you are finished reading this book, turn to the next-to-last page for **Text-Dependent Questions** and an **Extension Activity**.

TABLE OF CONTENTS

WHAT WILL ANNIE BE?

Annie Easley thought school was fun. Her only problem was "talking back." She sometimes had to stay after school when she did that. She didn't mean to cause trouble. She just had **opinions**, and she liked to share them.

Annie was born in 1933 in Birmingham, Alabama. Few African-American girls went to college then. But Annie's mother said, "You can be anything you want to be." She added, "But you have to work at it."

Most working women with college degrees were nurses or teachers. Annie was good at math. Maybe she would become a nurse.

RMINGHAM

LABAMA

Annie studied pharmacy in college. That is the study of medicines. Then she got married. She and her husband moved to Cleveland, Ohio. Annie thought she would keep studying pharmacy.

The pharmacy school there had closed. What could she do?

Cleveland

OHIO

Annie read an article about twin sisters who were "computers." They worked at a **research** lab. The work sounded interesting. The lab needed people who were good at math. Annie was good at math. Two weeks later, Annie began work at the lab. That was in 1955.

The Place for Space
Annie worked for a government group. It later became NASA. That stands for the National Aeronautics and Space Administration.

ANNIE THE COMPUTER

As a computer, Annie worked for researchers. She solved math problems. She figured out the answers by hand. She was good at the math, but work was not always fun. Only four African Americans worked there. They were not treated fairly. One time all the workers posed for a photo. Annie's face was cut out before the photo was displayed. That hurt her feelings.

Annie did not let this **bias** stop her. She said, "If I can't work with you, I will work around you. I was not about to ... walk away. That may be a solution for some people, but it's not mine."

Later, machines called computers were invented. People still needed to tell the machines what to do. Annie learned to use the machines. She became a computer programmer. She wrote **code** that made the machines run.

Her computer code helped with many NASA projects. One project sent rockets into space! She wrote many papers about rocket engines.

Annie also studied how to get power to vehicles. Her work on batteries helped make **hybrid** cars. Her other studies compared solar and wind energy.

Smaller and Faster
The first computers were machines that filled huge rooms. Over time, computers got smaller. They also got faster and more powerful. Much later, people got computers for home use. Now we have tiny computers in phones and watches.

Annie never stopped learning. In the 1970s, she went back to school. She earned a **degree** in mathematics. NASA paid for some employees to take classes. They would not pay for Annie's classes. She went anyway.

"You don't let it stop you," she said. "I'm able to take care of myself."

Annie helped others learn too. She tutored children in elementary and high school. She visited colleges. There she talked to students about working at NASA. She inspired students to try science and math careers.

MAKING WORK FAIR

Annie also fought for fair treatment at work. She **counseled** people who faced bias at work. They might have suffered unfair treatment because of their race, sex, or age. She helped find solutions.

"Nothing was given to minorities or women," she said. "It took some fighting." Annie was always ready to work for what she wanted.

Time for Play
Annie found time for fun. She ran and played tennis and golf. She helped start NASA's ski club. She set up employee picnics and a Christmas play for children. "Working was not my whole world," she said.

Life was changing for working women. Most of them wore dresses or skirts at work. One day Annie and another woman agreed to wear pantsuits. This let all the women know they could wear pants. Annie said, "We took the emphasis off what you're wearing. It's more like what you're actually producing."

Change did not happen as fast as Annie wanted. Still, she said, "I'm glad to have lived in this time. My good memories still outweigh the bad."

Diversity Makes a Difference
Now, one-third of NASA employees are women. Thousands come from diverse backgrounds. NASA supports diversity. They know having people of all types is important. Diversity leads to better ideas.

Annie broke down **barriers** for women and people of color. She did not plan to be a role model. But she inspired people through her talks. She brought enthusiasm to all she did. She lived by her mother's words: "You can be anything you want to be, but you have to work at it."

Inspiring Others

Annie Easley retired from NASA in 1989. She still often talked to young people. She encouraged them to go into math, science, and technology. She passed away in 2011. She was 78.

Annie wanted to do math. So she did.

"Don't listen to people who always tell you it's hard," Annie said. "Don't give up on it. Just stick with it."

TIME LINE

1933: Annie Easley is born on April 23.

1952: Annie studies pharmacy in college.

1954: Annie marries. She works as a substitute teacher.

1955: Annie gets a job as a "computer."

1957: The Soviet Union launches Sputnik. The space race begins.

1958: NACA becomes NASA.

1960s: Annie becomes a computer programmer.

1960s–1970s: Annie works on rocket systems.

1970s: Annie studies solar and wind energy.

1977: Annie gets a college degree in mathematics.

1989: Annie retires from NASA.

1997: The Cassini spacecraft is launched to Saturn. Annie worked on an early version of its rocket.

2011: Annie dies on June 25 at age 78.

GLOSSARY

barriers (BAIR-ee-urs): things that make progress hard

bias (BYE-uhs): unfairly helping or hurting a person or group

code (kode): instructions written for a computer

counseled (KOUN-suhld): gave help or advice

degree (di-GREE): a title given to a student who has finished a course of study

hybrid (HYE-brid): mixed; a hybrid car uses two forms of power

opinions (uh-PIN-yuhnz): feelings or beliefs

research (REE-surch): concerned with careful study of a subject to learn new facts

INDEX

TEXT-DEPENDENT QUESTIONS

1. How did Annie's mother inspire her?
2. How was Annie treated at work?
3. What happened when NASA got computer machines?
4. Why did Annie wear pants to work one day?
5. How did Annie inspire children?

EXTENSION ACTIVITY

Research the history of computers. How have they changed over time? How were they first used? How are they used now? What had to change? Imagine computers in the future. What do you think they will be like? Will they be used in new ways? Design a computer you would like to have when you grow up.

ABOUT THE AUTHOR

M.M. Eboch also writes books as Chris Eboch. History is one of her favorite subjects. Her book *The Eyes of Pharaoh* is a mystery in ancient Egypt. *The Well of Sacrifice* is a Mayan adventure. She lives in New Mexico with her husband and their two ferrets.

ABOUT THE ILLUSTRATOR

Elena Bia was born in a little town in northern Italy, near the Alps. In her free time, she puts her heart into personal comics. She also loves walking on the beach and walking through the woods. For her, flowers are the most beautiful form of life.

www.rourkeeducationalmedia.com

PHOTO CREDITS: Page 26: ©NASA
Quote sources: NASA: Annie Easley, Computer Scientist; https://www.nasa.gov/feature/annie-easley-computer-scientist; NASA Headquarters Oral History Project, Edited Oral History Transcript; https://www.jsc.nasa.gov/history/oral_histories/NASA_HQ/Herstory/EasleyAJ/EasleyAJ_8-21-01.htm; Annie Easley helped make modern spaceflight possible https://www.engadget.com/2015/02/13/annie-easley/

Edited by: Kim Thompson
Cover and interior design by: Rhea Magaro-Wallace

Library of Congress PCN Data

Annie Easley / M.M. Eboch
 (Women in Science and Technology)
  ISBN 978-1-73161-431-5 (hard cover)
  ISBN 978-1-73161-226-7 (soft cover)
  ISBN 978-1-73161-536-7 (e-Book)
  ISBN 978-1-73161-641-8 (ePub)
Library of Congress Control Number: 2019932137

Rourke Educational Media
Printed in the United States of America,
North Mankato, Minnesota